Away We Go!

John F. Loeper

Away We Go!

On Bicycles in 1898

ILLUSTRATED WITH OLD PRINTS

ATHENEUM : New York 1982

For Jane

LIBRARY OF CONGRESS CATALOGING IN PUBLICATION DATA

Loeper, John J.   Away we go!

SUMMARY: Discusses the history of the bicycle,
including the popularity it enjoyed during the 1890's.
Also examines other types of cycles, cycle racing, cycling
organizations, and related topics.
1. Cycling—History—19th century—Juvenile literature.
2. Bicycles—History—19th century—Juvenile literature.
[1. Bicycles and bicycling—History] I. Title
GV1040.5.L62   796.6   81-8045
ISBN 0-689-30884-1   AACR2

1|83 - JEUBE- 647|995

Published simultaneously in Canada by
McClelland & Stewart, Ltd.
Manufactured by American Book–Stratford Press,
Saddle Brook, New Jersey
Designed by M.M. Ahern
First Edition

Contents

BICYCLE OF 1876

"Straddle a Saddle"

Early bicycles were ridiculed as "boneshakers." And because they became a fad among fashionable young men, they were jokingly called "dandy horses."

How to ride a bicycle? asked one writer, laughing. "Just straddle a saddle, then paddle and skedaddle."

Yet, despite such ridicule, cycling caught America's fancy. The period between 1890 and 1900 saw millions of Americans, both young and old, "straddling the saddle." By this time the bicycle had been perfected. Little more would be done to improve its basic design or construction. These years have been called "The Golden Age of the Bicycle."

In 1900, the United States census claimed that few articles ever used by man had created so great a revolution in social behavior as the bicycle.

The bicycle craze of the 1890s ended with the arrival of the automobile. Then around 1960, the bicycle staged a comeback. And cycling is still growing in popularity. Today, more than eighty million cyclists in the United States are biking for health, recreation, and transportation. Millions more around the world ride bicycles.

Estimates indicate that every year more bicycles are sold than automobiles.

What is the attraction? A bicycle can become a part of you. It can be an extension of your arms and legs. It can take you to the store or carry you along the open road. It is a source of fun and adventure.

To find out about bikes and biking, let's "straddle the saddle" of history. We return to the golden age of the bicycle and join two boys in 1898.

A JOUST ON BICYCLES IN
LIVERPOOL, ENGLAND

"Away We Go!"

Morgan sat at the breakfast table with his parents. It was a beautiful spring morning in 1898. Outside, a cloudless sky and a soft breeze promised a spell of fair weather.

"Now, you be careful today!" his mother warned as she poured milk into his glass. "You and Jonah watch out for carriages.

"Yes, mother," Morgan answered.

"And don't ride too fast. You may hurt yourself."

"Listen to this," his father interrupted. He read aloud an item from the morning newspaper:

> Diamond Jim Brady, the millionaire playboy, presented the famous actress, Miss Lillian Russell, with a gold, jewel-encrusted bicycle. It has pearl handlebars and wheel spokes set with diamonds, rubies, and sapphires. It is reported to have cost over ten thousand dollars.

"Imagine that!" exclaimed Morgan's mother. "A jeweled bicycle!"

"I'd rather have my red one," Morgan said. His parents laughed.

Morgan had received a red Columbia Light Roadster for his eleventh birthday. This bike was manufactured by the Pope Company of Boston. Colonel Albert Pope and the company bearing his name began the manufacture of bicycles in 1877. The year before, the Colonel, a retired Civil War officer, had attended the 1876 Centennial Exhibition in Philadelphia. There he saw an English bicycle on display and decided to manufacture bicycles in America. Although not the first cycle manufacturer, Colonel Pope is considered the father of the American bicycle industry.

Though manufacture began earlier, it was really around 1890 that bicycling took hold in America. *Outing Magazine*, a popular publication of the period, said:

> The cycle trade is now one of the chief industries of the world. Since 1890, every season has witnessed a doubling of bicycle production. The supply is unequal to the demand.

The *Scientific American* added:

> The bicycle has put the human race on wheels.

Everyone bicycled: the young, the old, the rich, and the not so rich. Stage stars and millionaires took to the sport. The Vanderbilts and the Goulds ordered bikes. John D. Rockefeller presented bicycles to his friends. Tiffany's, the New York jeweler, offered sterling silver bicycles in its catalogue. The "cycling disease" even invaded Washington. Members of President McKinley's cabinet rode bicycles. And it was reported that Mr. Justice White of the Supreme Court was seen pedaling down Pennsylvania Avenue in his judicial robes.

While the nation's newspapers reported on this

"craziest craze of all," companies vied with each other in boasting about their bikes. Advertisements proclaimed "the joy of riding," the "ease of propulsion," and the "smooth ride."

Some were alarmed by the craze. Certain business-men worried that the bicycle would bring economic ruin. Piano and book sales slowed. A Chicago music store owner complained:

> It used to be that young couples saved up to buy
> a piano. Now they save to buy two bicycles.

Jewelers and watchmakers grumbled. Americans who had once bought watches for their children's birthdays now bought bicycles. Candy manufacturers joined in. Children saved their pennies to buy bicycle accessories instead of candy. Theater attendance fell. The *New York Journal of Commerce* summed it up by saying: "What is gain for the bicycle makers is a loss to other businessmen.

Like so many others, Morgan loved his bicycle. After breakfast, he went to the backyard shed where his bike was stored. He unlatched the door and wheeled out his red Columbia. It had a 23-inch frame, 28-inch wheels, pneumatic tires, and a chain drive. The bike had no brakes. Brakes were an option, and one had to pay extra for them. Braking was done by backpedaling or placing the sole of the foot against the front tire.

After polishing the frame of his Columbia with a flannel cloth, Morgan rode to his friend's house. Jonah lived two blocks away on Delaware Avenue.

The boys had planned their weekend bike hike one day during recess. They were going to take the Old Farm Road to Doylestown and return along the canal.

They were fortunate. Bicycles were expensive. Morgan's Columbia cost over 125 dollars. Jonah's bike, a Whitten Godding, cost 115 dollars. In 1898, one hundred dollars was the equivalent of more than eight hundred dollars today. To encourage sales, some bicycles were sold on the installment plan. This idea appeared around 1892. Half the price was paid as a down-payment, and the balance was paid in monthly installments. A Minnesota newspaper reported in 1895 that: "A great many bicycles have been purchased on the installment plan, and the buyers are keeping up with their payments."

The earliest bicycles, those sold in the 1860s, cost over three hundred dollars. Today, that would be almost three thousand dollars!

Nobody knows for certain who invented the bicycle. Ancient Egyptian drawings show a kind of wheeled contraption resembling a bicycle. And, a medieval stained glass window in an English church pictures an angel mounted on a bicycle-like vehicle. Most historians, however, credit the invention to a Frenchman, M. de Sivrac. In 1791, he mounted a wooden rail between two wheels. He sat on it and pushed it along with his feet. In 1816, a German, Baron von Drais, made an almost identical machine but his could be steered using the front wheel. The

Draisine made cycling popular. A Frenchman, Ernest Michaux, is given credit for the first successful pedal bicycle. As years passed, sprockets and a chain drive were added to Michaux's cycle. Improvements in design and construction occurred rapidly. By 1879 an Englishman, H. J. Lawson, designed the first rear-driving "safety" bicycle with chain transmission.

As Morgan turned the corner at Delaware Avenue, he saw Jonah astride his bike.

"Where have you been?" Jonah called out. "I've been waiting for you. Let's go!"

The two rode out of town and turned onto the Old Farm Road. Their bikes whizzed along. They rode humped over with their backs almost parallel to the road. Any boy who rode upright would have been called a sissy. It might be mentioned that many parents and doctors did not approve of such riding. Morgan's mother worried that her son might become a hunchback, victim of "bicycle hump." Medical journals warned against "dorsal curvature by biking," along with "bicycle hand" and "bicycle wrist" and "bicycle twitch." All these ailments were said to be caused by bicycling.

Not sharing these fears, Morgan and Jonah pedaled along. They were on their bikes and looking forward to a day of fun.

"Away we go!" Morgan shouted.

"Dang Bicycles!"

The Old Farm Road, a dirt lane, led from the village of Well's Ferry to Doylestown. Tradition claimed that the road was an old Indian trail.

Bicycles were permitted on the Farm Road. This was not generally true. The first machine to provoke pedestrians, panic horses, and incur hatred was not the automobile. It was the bicycle. State laws gave local authorities the power to regulate bicycle use. In some instances, cyclists were forbidden the use of public roads. Illinois proposed legislation that would compel a cyclist to dismount when meeting a horse. In other parts of the country, cyclists were held responsible for damages that resulted when horses became frightened of their bikes. Cyclists were objects of discrimination. In 1883 New York City refused cyclists the use of paths in Central Park. In New Jersey authorities banned cyclists on the turnpikes. At that time turnpikes were simply cross-state roads used by horse and carriage. Cyclists fought these rules and, later on, many were revoked.

Many people resented bicycles despite their popularity. Often, mean farmers took delight in blocking roads or going along slowly in their wagons just to irritate cyclists

behind them. The story is told of one wagon driver who enjoyed spitting tobacco juice on passing cyclists. Pranksters thrust sticks between the spokes of wheels to knock cyclists off their seats. In New England in 1897, a horse-driven vehicle deliberately careened into a group of cyclists, injuring many of the riders. Cyclists found antagonism everywhere. Some life insurance companies listed cycling as a "hazardous occupation," which forced cyclists to pay a double premium. Through bicycle organizations, the cyclists fought for fair play.

"Let's stop a while. I'm getting tired!" Jonah called to Morgan.

The two brought their bikes to a halt. They rolled them onto the edge of a field and sat down on a rise of grass. The morning sun burned brightly.

"When we get to Doylestown, I'll treat you to some candy," Morgan said. "I have money with me." He fished into a trouser pocket and pulled out a handful of pennies.

"Boy!" Jonah exclaimed. "You're rich!"

"Here, let's count them," Morgan said.

The boys began to count their coins. Suddenly they were interrupted by a loud voice.

"Get those dang bi-sigh-cles out of here!"

Looking up, they confronted an angry man.

At first, no one was sure how to pronounce the word. Some said bi-sigh-cle. Others said bi-sick-le. Over the years the latter pronunciation won out.

"I don't want any wheeled contraptions around here," the man continued.

"But bicycles are allowed on this road," Morgan protested.

"On the road, yes. But not in my field!" the man scolded. "Get them out and keep them out!"

Obediently the boys removed their bicycles. As they walked their bikes along the road, they heard a bell tinkle. A young woman rode by on a tricycle. She rang her bell again as she passed by.

Some riders considered the conventional bicycle a bit too dangerous or too undignified. They felt safer on a tricycle. The three wheels offered better balance and an

easier ride. The early tricycles had two high rear wheels and a third steering wheel in front. The driver sat suspended between the rear wheels.

Not only were there bicycles (two wheels) and tricycles (three wheels) but also unicycles (one wheel). Riding a unicycle requires a good sense of balance. The rider literally walks on a wheel. The unicycle is considered a stunt bike by many cyclists, rather than a means of transportation.

Since its invention, many variations of the bicycle have appeared. In 1895 one man built tricycle roller skates. These were miniature tricycles strapped to shoes. Another inventor designed a bicycle with wooden runners attached alongside the wheels. He claimed his "snow bike" could be pedaled over snow and ice.

The Well's Ferry Touring Club

"I guess our rest break is over," Jonah said. "We better get going."

The boys mounted their bikes and rode off. It was a glorious day. With a blue sky overhead and a hard road beneath, they needed nothing else. It was a day made for biking.

"What's that?" Jonah called out.

"What?" Morgan answered.

"That noise," Jonah said.

They brought their bikes to a stop and looked behind them. A swirl of dust in the distance caught their attention. They heard shouting and a hum of wheels.

"It's the Well's Ferry Touring Club!" Morgan said.

The popularity of the bicycle during the 1890s brought about the formation of bicycle clubs. People in towns and cities joined together to share the fun of cycling. The clubs sponsored races, picnics, rallies, and tours. Even high society joined in. An exclusive bicycle club in Chicago held "bicycle dances." Members cycled in a ballroom to the strains of waltz music. The Michaux Club of New York City was housed in an elegant three-storied mansion. It had a huge riding rink. Visitors could watch riders circle around from balconies, while waiters served them food and drink. Both male and female members of the Michaux Club wore a prescribed uniform. The men were outfitted in white knickers, red coats, red stockings, and white shoes. The ladies wore white skirts, red-and-white striped shirts, white shoes, and a straw hat. Members' bicycles were decorated with red and white ribbons. The Boston Bicycle Club dressed in brown and silver.

Clubs were everywhere. Every American town and village seemed to have one. There were even specialty clubs. A Fat Man's Bicycle Club was organized in Brooklyn. Members had to weigh over two hundred fifty pounds. Philadelphia boasted a Chinese Bicycling Club, and there was an all-Japanese group in New York—the Rising Sun Bicycle Club.

Miss Polly Pettipoint was the founder and president of the Well's Ferry Touring Club. An enthusiastic bicyclist, she was the proud owner of a five foot high "penny-farthing."

In 1876, the penny-farthing (named after an English coin) appeared at the Philadelphia Centennial Exhibition.

It was also known as the "high wheeler." Invented in England, it had a very large front wheel and a small rear wheel. The large wheel supposedly allowed better speed.

Miss Pettipoint had ordered an American version of the penny-farthing. It was a high wheeler manufactured by Clark Cycle Company of Baltimore.

She agreed with *Outing Magazine*. It called cycling "a step toward the emancipation of women." In a speech before a Well's Ferry Women's club, Miss Pettipoint promoted her organization. "Cycling will build up your feeble frames," she told the women, quoting a cycling authority. "It will rid you of dull, unhappy thoughts."

During the 1890s, more and more women came to regard the bicycle as a means of freedom. No longer content to stay at home, women took to the roads on bikes. A midwestern newspaper of the period commented:

> Cycling is bringing about a change of feeling regarding woman and her capabilities. A woman awheel is an independent creature, free to go where she wants. Before the bicycle, this freedom was denied her.

The sound of shouting and laughter told Morgan and Jonah that the Touring Club was having a race.

"I'll bet Miss Pettipoint is up front on her highwheeler," Jonah said. Sure enough, as the cyclists approached, Miss Pettipoint was leading the way. She was quite a sight perched high above the front wheel of her penny-farthing. She wore an ankle-length dress, leather boots, and a wide-brimmed straw hat.

Behind her were other cyclists intent on keeping up with their leader. Holding up the rear was Grandpa Perry, his gray whiskers glistening with perspiration. Although he huffed and puffed, Grandpa was convinced that cycling was good for his health.

Many doctors of the time encouraged cycling. They claimed that it drove away headaches, sleeplessness, and rheumatism. One prominent physician announced that "cycling is a tonic, giving a vigorous tone to the whole system."

As he pedaled by, Grandpa Perry waved to the two boys.

"Why not join us?" he shouted.

"Come on," said Morgan. "Let's go with them!"

Morgan and Jonah hopped on their bikes and followed along. They stayed at the rear keeping company with Grandpa.

As they rolled along, the grade increased. They were approaching the climb up Jerico Mountain. Morgan and Jonah found the pedaling difficult. Grandpa pushed and strained. With each push the wheels turned more slowly.

"Let's walk our bikes up the hill," Morgan suggested.

"No sir!" Grandpa exclaimed. "No dang mountain will stop me!"

"But Grandpa, it's too steep!" Jonah argued.

"You ought to be ashamed of yourself!" Grandpa scolded. "Look at Miss Pettipoint tackle this hill! And she's a lot older than you!"

Jonah and Morgan smiled. Grandpa was right. Miss Pettipoint was still up front. Head down, her skirt flapped in rhythm with each turn of the high wheel.

"Keep pedaling!" Grandpa ordered.

Their legs ached, but they kept the wheels in motion.

Before long, they had crested the mountain.

"We did it!" Grandpa shouted in triumph. "The rest of the way is easy! It's downhill all the way to Doylestown!"

As any bike rider knows, going downhill is the most fun. No pedaling is required; you simply give way to the pull of gravity.

At the time in Montana, trolley cars took cyclists and their bicycles up into the mountains. The cyclists had the comfort of riding up the mountainside, then cycling downhill. It worked rather like a ski lift.

A contemporary poet wrote:

> *Faster, faster, what a thrill,*
> *Cycling down a country hill.*
> *No need for effort, nor for care,*
> *Just coast along as fast as air.*

A BICYCLE OF THE FUTURE?

Charlie's Ghost

Morgan and Jonah were in no hurry. They decided to take another short rest stop. Waving goodbye to Grandpa, they sat down by the roadside. The trees on the mountaintop shaded the road and obscured the sky. It was all woodland, with no houses in sight.

"It's so quiet, it's kinda spooky," Jonah said.

"I hear tell that there's a ghost up here," Morgan offered.

"What kind of a ghost?" Jonah asked.

"My Aunt Polly says that years ago an old hermit lived up here in a shack. Everyone said he was crazy. Fact is, they called him Crazy Charlie. He died and his ghost still haunts the mountaintop."

"Well, I don't believe your Aunt Polly," Jonah said. "And I don't believe in ghosts!"

"It's true," Morgan insisted. "Aunt Polly says that lots of folks have seen and heard him. He always asks in a ghostly voice, 'Who's on my mountain?'"

"Don't believe it!" Jonah exclaimed.

He had no sooner finished speaking then the boys heard a rustle of leaves.

"What's that?" Jonah asked.

"Probably just a rabbit," Morgan told his friend.

"You don't think it's Crazy Charlie's ghost?"

"I thought you didn't believe in ghosts!" Morgan taunted.

There was another rustle. Then Morgan called out. "Look over there!" He pointed to a small clearing in the woods. There, amid tall grass and weeds, were the remains of a wooden shack.

"It must be Crazy Charlie's place!" Morgan whispered. With that, a ghostly voice called out, "Who-o-o."

"Let's go!" Jonah said. The two jumped on their bikes and started off. They had gone only a short distance when a dark figure swooped across their path.

"It's Crazy Charlie's ghost!" Jonah cried out.

"It's an owl!" Morgan laughed.

Jonah pedaled as fast as he could. The downhill slope increased his speed.

As his bike whizzed away, Morgan called out.

"You'll break a world speed record, Jonah! And you'll owe it all to Charlie's ghost!"

From its earliest days, the bicycle has been used for racing. The first recorded bicycle race was held in France in 1868. That same year, the first race in America was held at the Empire Skating Rink in New York City. By the 1890s six-day bicycle races were being held at Madison Square Garden in New York. The first six-day race, held in 1891 at the Garden, was won by "Plugger" Martin. He pedaled 1,466 miles during the six days.

Perhaps the greatest bicycle racer of all time was A. A. Zimmerman. He is still talked about today. In 1891 he recorded a world record for the half-mile. Riding a high-wheeled "ordinary," he made it in one minute ten seconds.

Another famous name in cycling history belonged to a black cyclist, Marshall Taylor. This cyclist set records in almost every distance race—the quarter mile, the half mile, the one- and two-mile races—during the late 1890s.

Perhaps the most colorful racer was Mile-a-Minute Murphy. He earned his nickname by cycling a mile in less than sixty seconds.

At the foot of Jerico Mountain, the two bikes coasted to a halt. There, in a field near Tomkin's Farm, the boys found the Well's Ferry Touring Club enjoying a picnic lunch. Miss Pettipoint saw them and called out.

"Come join us, boys. We have plenty of food. Mrs. Tomkin prepared a picnic for us."

Morgan and Jonah were delighted to accept. They were hungry. Joining the group, they feasted on sandwiches, lemonade, and big wedges of cherry pie.

Between gulps of lemonade, Jonah told Grandpa Perry about the ghost.

"It was just an owl!" Morgan insisted.

"Was it gray?" Grandpa asked.

Jonah nodded his head.

"Did it swoop down out of nowhere?"

Another nod.

"Did it say 'Who-o-o'?"

His eyes widened. Jonah shook his head again.

"Then I'm sure that was Charlie's ghost!" Grandpa chuckled.

An Angry Dog

Leaving the Touring Club to its outdoor festivities, after thanking them for lunch, Morgan and Jonah went on their way. They pedaled down the road toward Doylestown.

A short distance away, the road curved by Tomkin's Farm. As they passed the barn, they heard a sharp bark. A flock of chickens scattered and a fuzzy white dog darted from behind the barn. He was small with a black spot over one eye, undoubtedly a mongrel. The animal scurried toward them, yapping fiercely. He ran after them, snapping at the wheels of the bikes.

"Get out of here!" Morgan ordered.

"Go away, mutt!" Jonah added.

But the dog persisted. He continued barking and snapping at the wheels. The boys pedaled faster. Then, with a leap, the little dog grabbed hold of Morgan's stocking. Thrown off balance, the bike and Morgan toppled over. Jonah stopped short and jumped off his bike.

"Scat!" he shouted at the dog, clapping his hands.

The animal looked at him for a moment, growled, then turned and ran off.

"Are you all right?" Jonah asked.

"I think so," Morgan answered, brushing himself off.

A dog may be man's best friend, but there's something about a person on a bicycle that brings out the worst in a dog. Dogs have always caused problems for cyclists. In 1893, the Ki-Yi gun was invented. Like a water pistol, it squirted liquid ammonia at a dog. It didn't hurt him, but the strong smell chased him away. Some

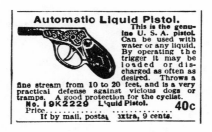

Automatic Liquid Pistol. This is the genuine U. S. A. pistol. Can be used with water or any liquid. By operating the trigger it may be loaded or discharged as often as desired. Throws a fine stream from 10 to 20 feet, and is a very practical defense against vicious dogs or tramps. A good protection for the cyclist.
No. 19K2229 L'quid Pistol. 40c
Price..........
If by mail, postal extra, 9 cents.

early cyclists carried ground pepper with them to throw at angry dogs. Other animals disliked bicycles too. Often, goats and bulls chased after bikes. A story is even told of a raccoon who chased after a bike.

The many rough roads of the period, antagonistic farmers, and angry animals made cycling somewhat dangerous. The *Encyclopedia of Special Information and Treasury of Useful Knowledge* offered this advice in 1885:

> Riding on a bicycle can be different and bring
> the rider to face with many dangers. To prepare
> for bicycling follow the rules of regular rest
> and a proper diet. The daily use of a cold bath

cannot be too strongly insisted upon; also early rising and an early bedtime. Avoid rich foods, such as pork, veal, duck, salmon and pastry. Vegetables, coffee and tea should be taken in moderation. A good bodily condition is required for the habitual bicycle rider.

Many doctors warned against riding on a full stomach. One recommended "a little bread and a glass of warm milk" as a suitable breakfast before cycling. Generally, doctors approved of cycling although not all were convinced of its benefits. One warned that excessive cycling might lead to insanity.

"That darn dog!" Morgan uttered. The rear wheel guard of his red Columbia was slightly scratched.

"A touch of paint will fix that," Jonah consoled.

They remounted their bikes and went on. In the distance they could see the rooftops of Doylestown.

"I'm looking forward to that candy you promised me," Jonah said.

"After all that pie you ate at the picnic!" Morgan joked.

"There's always room for candy!" Jonah answered.

Dietary rules for cyclists meant nothing to Jonah!

A Bicycle Built
for Two

After buying and eating two bags of penny candy at the
Doylestown Candy Palace, Morgan and Jonah rode out
of town toward the canal. It was early afternoon and a
blazing sun filtered through the trees lining the roadway.

This was a busier route than the Farm Road. It was
crowded with horse-drawn carriages and wagons. The
boys were cautious. They did not want a startled horse
to bolt. If this happened, they might be ordered off the
road.

Near Bogart's Tavern, about three miles from town,
they passed a female cyclist wearing newfangled bloomers. The boys giggled at what seemed an outlandish
outfit.

The popularity of the bicycle brought many daring and
unusual fashions. For women, cycling was emancipating.
More simple clothing was introduced. Hoopskirts and
other awkward attire gave way to short skirts, bloomers,
and culottes. These gave more freedom of movement

while riding and in getting on and off bicycles. Still, it was women's clothing that caused the top tube bar on bicycles to be lowered. This is why we have the so-called "girl's bike."

In 1892, the Lady Cyclists Association recommended "rational dress" for biking. They suggested wearing a pair of dark stockings and a pair of loose knickers fastened with an elastic band under the knee. A contemporary account gives this description of a female cyclist:

Here was an elderly lady on a bicycle, wearing a pair of baggy knickers reaching below the knee and a jacket which fell over her hips. On her head she wore a flat, brimmed hat covered with ribbons and her feet were encased in high, leather boots.

Some people were shocked by these styles. A social reporter wrote in a city newspaper:

I hope that this silly clothing will soon disappear.

In Long Island, teachers were forbidden to ride bicycles to school. The reason was given by the school superintendent:

It is not proper for ladies to ride bicycles. They will want to be in style and wear bloomers. How would our schoolrooms look with lady teachers parading about in bloomers. They might as well wear men's trousers.

The combination of liberated fashions and excessive biking caused concern among churches, too. One minister warned, "You cannot serve God and skylark on a bicycle!"

A Methodist church in New Jersey voted to expel any member who rode a bicycle on Sunday. Another church made its members promise, "I will not ride my wheel on the Sabbath and will try to discourage others in the use of the Sunday wheel." In 1885, a young lady questioned a magazine about bicycling on Sunday. She received the following advice:

> If it is the only means of reaching the church for service, then bicycling on Sunday is allowed.

Ladies' Bicycle Leggins.

No. 31514. Ladies' Canvas Bicycle Leggins, very fine, in fact, look like a fine black button, knee length, with 9 buttons and buckle at top. Sizes, 2½ to 7; weight, 7 oz. Colors, black or brown.
Per pair.......**$0.40**

This same magazine suggested that ladies should ride a bike sidesaddle. It gave these "simple" instructions for mounting the bicycle:

First vault the bicycle in the usual way and work up to a moderate speed. Then, delicately place the right leg over the seat and continue pedaling with the left.

Not many female cyclists accepted the suggestion.

Morgan and Jonah biked on. The road was level, and the biking easy. They sat bent forward. This is the most comfortable and least tiring position. With the body at a forty-five degree angle, a bicyclist's weight is distributed more evenly over the vehicle. The cyclist is much more relaxed and wind resistance is lowered.

Going by Peter's Corners, they passed other cyclists on a tandem bike. It was an amusing sight.

A tandem is a "bicycle built for two." The machine rides two people sitting one behind the other, both pedaling in unison. The front handlebars control the steering. This double bicycle held a fat gentleman with a large mustache and a young lady wearing a floppy straw hat.

A popular song of the period romanticized the tandem:

Daisy, Daisy, give me your answer true,
I'm half crazy over the love of you.
It won't be a stylish marriage,
I can't afford a carriage,
But you'll look sweet
Upon the seat
Of a bicycle built for two.

There were even variations of the tandem. Some three and four seaters were manufactured. But perhaps the most remarkable multi-seated bike was made in England. It held twenty riders; was over thirty-five feet long, and weighed nearly one thousand pounds. Still another unusual tandem was the "Eiffel Tower Bike." Built in 1896, its elevated front seat was twenty feet high.

Beyond Peter's Corners, the boys reached the canal and towpath. Barges laden with coal and freight were pulled along this waterway by mules who trudged the towpath alongside the canal. The towpath made a perfect bicycle path and led right into Well's Ferry. By now, Morgan and Jonah were hot and growing tired. They had traveled a number of miles and the late afternoon temperature was climbing.

"Let's take a break," Morgan suggested.

Jonah agreed, and the two found a thick patch of cool grass.

Cooling Off

"I'm hot!" Jonah complained.

"Then, let's take a swim," Morgan suggested.

Within minutes, the boys had stripped off their clothing and jumped into the canal. The water was delightful.

The overhanging trees and thick foliage along the canal gave them complete privacy. The only intruder was a rabbit who, for a moment, hopped along the towpath, then disappeared into the bushes. They splashed about for a long while enjoying the water. Refreshed, they climbed up to the towpath and dried themselves with their shirts. Again, they sat down on the grass.

"I got the latest copy of the *Journal*," Morgan said. "It has an article on Tom Stevens and his adventures."

The American Bicycling Journal was published in Boston. It cost ten cents a copy and appeared every other Saturday. The *Journal* was the first and most popular biking magazine in the country.

The article Morgan mentioned was about Thomas

Stevens. He was the first man to cycle from coast to coast. In 1884 this twenty-nine-year-old rode, shoved, and hauled an "ordinary" high-wheeled bicycle from California to Boston, Massachusetts. Maps were unknown, so he had only a slight idea of the route he would have to follow. He crossed rivers and mountains and pushed his way through snowdrifts. He was forced to carry his bike through miles of soft sand in Nevada. He crossed the Rockies and pedaled through the grasslands. Stevens arrived in Boston in August of 1884.

The following year, Stevens undertook a more ambitious venture. He decided to continue around the world on his two-wheeled machine. He bicycled across the continents of Europe and Asia to China. Then, he sailed to Japan; crossed that country, and sailed to San Francisco. When his trip ended in 1886, he had biked over 13,000 miles. Stevens' trip was financed by Col. Albert Pope, the bicycle manufacturer. His lonely and often hazardous journey was a true adventure and captured the imagination of millions.

There were other cross-country and around-the-world trips by bicycle. In 1894, a young American girl set out to tour the world. Annie Londonberry set out one July morning to cycle around the globe. Another famous woman cyclist was Fannie Bullock Workman, the daughter of a governor of Massachusetts. Mrs. Workman spent ten years touring the world on her bicycle. She published three books on her adventures. Another woman, Margaret LeLong, took off on her bicycle in 1896. Against the advice of family and friends, she pedaled westward from Chicago to San Francisco.

Such long distance biking was much admired by cycling enthusiasts, and the riders were hailed as heroes and heroines.

"Imagine biking across the country. Eighteen eighty-four was a long time ago, but it would still be an adventure!" Jonah remarked.

"The magazine article tells about a lot of things that happened to him," Jonah continued. "A bunch of cowboys shot bullets at him, and he was chased by a pack of coyotes."

"Wow!" Jonah exclaimed.

The afternoon sun sat low in the western sky, casting long shadows across the canal.

"I've had fun today," Jonah said.

"Me, too," Morgan answered. "But, we better start home. It's getting late."

Back on their bikes, the boys continued along the canal. The riding was easy. The towpath was worn smooth and hard by the barge mules. And of course, to make it even easier, the boys' enjoyed the luxury of pneumatic tires.

The pneumatic tire was the invention of an Irish veterinarian, John Dunlop. He conceived the idea of fitting an inflated rubber hose around the wheels of his son's bicycle. The idea brought him great fame. It revolutionized bicycle riding, because it permitted a far more comfortable ride. This was appreciated on the rough and rutted roads bicyclists of the past had to use.

Along the way, Morgan and Jonah saw a barge coming toward them.

"Better walk our bikes so the mule can get by," Morgan called out.

The young mule, head bent, walked along pulling a coal barge behind him. The rope connecting mule and barge was taut.

"Get out of the way, boys!" a man's voice called out. "Daffodil doesn't like bicycles."

A man on the barge waved his arms. He was right. When the mule, Daffodil, noticed the bicycles, it stopped and brayed. "He-haw! He-haw! He-haw! the animal bellowed.

"Go into the bushes!" the man shouted.

The two boys wheeled their bikes behind a spreading honeysuckle. Daffodil wiggled its ears. Certain that the offending bicycles were gone, it moved on. The barge glided behind.

"Daffodil was once frightened by a bicycle," the barge man explained as he rode by. "And a mule never forgets!"

Morgan and Jonah waited until Daffodil was out of sight before moving on. By now the sun was moving toward the horizon.

"We better hurry," Morgan said. "I'll be in trouble if I'm late for supper!"

"And I'm so hungry, I could eat a mule," Jonah told him.

Scorcher

The towpath led the boys into Well's Ferry. The canal followed through the heart of the village.

As they pedaled under the Main Street bridge, the clock in the church tower struck six. Climbing off their bikes, they rolled them up a path leading to the street.

Coming toward them, down Main Street, was the Well's Ferry Touring Club. They were also returning from their day's outing. Miss Pettipoint was still leading the way on her high-wheeler, and Grandpa Perry was still at the rear.

Seeing the boys, the club members waved and called out.

"It's been a wonderful day on wheels!" Miss Pettipoint shouted. The members were on their way to the Church Hall, the club's headquarters.

"Humbug!" snarled Grandpa Perry as he rolled by.

Later, the boys learned that Grandpa had had an encounter with a Dolyestown policeman, and had been fined for "disturbing the peace of a public highway." It seems that Grandpa had hit a bump and lost control of his steering. His bike wobbled and wiggled across the road until it bumped into a horse and buggy. The horse, a timid old mare, became frightened and bolted. The driver had been furious and called a policeman. Grandpa had had to pay a two-dollar fine and listen to a lecture on "scorching."

A bicycle speeder or reckless driver was called a "scorcher." Although not used today, the word was very common in the 1890s. While he was governor of New York, Teddy Roosevelt was called a "scorcher" by the newspapers for his "reckless spending of tax money." It was not a complimentary word. Grandpa was insulted.

Nonetheless, careless cyclists could be something of a problem. In 1896 a Chicago newspaper wrote:

> As a source of accidents, the cycle knows no rival. The three leading causes of accidents are scorching, beginning drivers, and just plain stupid driving.

Many of the accidents were the result of competition for streets and highways. Wagons, streetcars, carts, and carriages crowded the roadways. To streets already crowded came the bicycles. And those who were there before didn't like it.

As mentioned before, cyclists wanted to establish their right to use their vehicles wherever they liked. They wanted the use of highways without fear of being prose-

ON WHEELS THROUGH GOLDEN GATE PARK

cuted. So they formed biking associations to pressure local and state governments into recognizing their rights. Often, women cyclists were dragged into court to be accused not only of careless cycling, but also of "improper dress and conduct unbecoming a lady." So cycling groups came out in strong defense of women's rights.

They also insisted on more and better roads. The rutted roads of the period could send a rider flying through the air. Through their efforts, roads were improved. In 1895, twin bicycle paths were opened in Brooklyn from Prospect Park to Coney Island. And, in California, a Cycleway was constructed from Pasadena to Los Angeles.

All across the country, the new sport was bringing improvements. In many different ways, the bicycle contributed to modern transportation. Many of the pioneer automobile inventors were bicycle mechanics. In Germany, Gottlieb Daimler and Karl Benz constructed motorized bikes before they built automobiles. In America, the Chevrolet brothers and other automotive pioneers first worked with bikes.

Wilbur and Orville Wright designed their historic flying machine in their bicycle shop. The poet, John Dos Passos said:

The chilly December day
two shivering bicycle mechanics
from Dayton, Ohio,

first felt their homemade contraption
whittled out of hickory sticks,
gummed together with Arnstein's bicycle cement.

"Poor Grandpa!" Jonah remarked. "Called a 'scorcher' by a policeman!"

"And a two-dollar fine!" Morgan added.

"Maybe the Touring Club will do something about it," Jonah said. "After all, it was just an accident."

Journey's End

"I had fun today," Jonah said.

"Me, too," Morgan answered.

"Next weekend, let's go to the park and play soldier," Jonah suggested.

"Swell!" Morgan agreed. "We can ask Tom and Dan to join us. They have bikes. You can be the general, and I'll be your lieutenant. Tom and Dan can play the enemy."

The plans were exciting. That was the fun of bicycling. You could do so many things. The main difference between cycling in the 1890s and now is that bicycles then were the fastest wheels on the road. The thrill of speed and adventure kept people pedaling. There seemed no end to the possibilities of the bicycle.

In an issue of *Harper's Magazine*, it was suggested that "the bicycle will find its highest function in time of war. On bicycles, soldiers can move in any direction with ease and speed."

The notion was quickly accepted. In America, the

FRANCE—THE INTRODUCTION OF BICYCLES
INTO THE ARMY

first branch of the military to use bicycles was the National
Guard of Connecticut. Soon after, the United States Sig-
nal Corps employed bikes, some with guns mounted on
the handlebars. Between 1890 and 1900, large numbers
of soldiers learned to ride and drill on bicycles. A group
of soldier-cyclists was formed called the United States

Military Wheelmen. Lieutenant Whitney, of this group, claimed, "We are told somewhere that for the want of a horseshoe nail a battle was lost. In the next war, for want of a bicycle the independence of a nation may be lost."

In 1894 a meeting of National Guard representatives in Denver predicted that there would soon be an army of over fifty thousand cycling soldiers. The first attempt to use bicycles in combat took place during the Spanish-American War in 1898. The attempt failed, and the predictions that the bicycle would be a military weapon died.

Plans made, the boys parted company to dream of imaginary battles and maneuvers in the park.

In the small towns of the 1890s, there was not much for children to do. There were no swimming pools or libraries or movie theaters. It was before the radio and television and before basketball and even baseball became popular. The bicycle craze of the 1890s may make us smile today. The notions about proper dress, cycling on Sunday, "scorching" and bicycle soldiers may seem foolish. Yet the bicycle was exciting and an important part of life. It brought fun and freedom; it let you go where you pleased. It was like having a legendary pair of seven-league boots to carry you away.

The enthusiasm for the bicycle died around 1900 with the arrival of the automobile. By the time Morgan and Jonah grew to adulthood, Americans had transferred their love for the bicycle to the automobile. Yet, the bicycle paved the way for the new transportation. It was cyclists who fought for better roads and helped to establish the rights of horseless vehicles.

The American bicycle industry survived by selling the bicycle as a toy. However, in Europe and other parts of the world, the vehicle retained its status as a means of transportation. Today, Americans have rediscovered the bicycle. Cycling has risen from near obscurity to a new popularity. The bicycle was and still is "that glorious contraption."

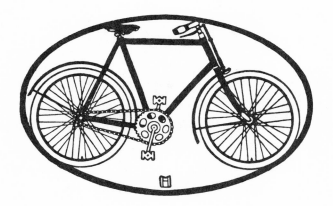

Bicycle Safety— Old & New

It has been estimated that over thirty-five thousand cyclists are injured each year in accidents. Most of these injuries are among children five to fourteen years old. Riding a bike carries with it certain responsibilities.

These tips on bicycle safety were published in an Indianian newspaper in June of 1894. They are as important to follow today as they were then:

1. Be courteous to pedestrians. Always give them the right of way.
2. Keep a good distance behind any carriage.
3. Slow down and look right and left at crossroads.
4. Make certain that your cycle is in working order.
5. Never do stunts with your cycle.
6. Never try to hitch a ride by holding onto a wagon.
7. Never ride two on a bike unless it is a tandem.

A SCHOOL IN NEW YORK FOR LEARNING
TO RIDE BICYCLES

8. Steer straight; don't weave.
9. Watch for dogs, other small animals, and young children.
10. Ride on the right and in a straight line. Stay close to the side of the road. Single file if in a group.

Bicycle Clubs

Like the Well's Ferry Touring Club of old, many bicycling groups exist in towns and cities today. There are also national and international organizations of cyclists. Among these are:

The League of American Wheelmen
P. O. Box 3919
Torrance, California 90510

During the early years of cycling, riders were called "wheelmen." When a group of cyclists banded together in 1880, it was only proper to call themselves The League of American Wheelmen.

One of the oldest cycling groups in America, the League sponsors local and national bicycling events and tours. Among its members were Orville and Wilbur Wright, Commodore Vanderbilt, and Diamond Jim Brady.

American Youth Hostels, Inc.
20 West 17th Street
New York, New York 10011

American Youth Hostels is an organization that offers the "young in spirit" a wide range of activities. The organization serves both individuals and groups. Many scout troop, schools, and clubs participate in AYH activities.

AYH operates hostels offering room and board for traveling cyclists. It organizes bicycling trips both in America and in Europe.

The International Bicycle Touring Society
846 Prospect St.
Lo Jolla, California 92037

Founded in 1964 by a California physician, Dr. Clifford Graves, this group sponsors bike tours with an emphasis on historic or cultural interest

Amateur Bicycle League of America
256th Street
Floral Park
Long Island, New York 11001

Founded in 1820, the ABL is the governing body of bicycle racing in the United States. It is a member of the U.S. Olympic Committee. ABL national championship races are held each year in late summer. Riders are selected to represent the United States in the Olympics.

Bicycle racing has been an Olympic event since 1896.

Victor Bicycles

~ For 1894. ~

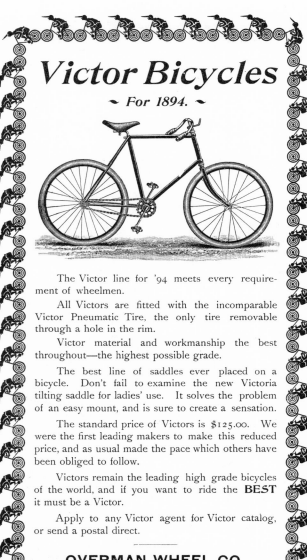

The Victor line for '94 meets every requirement of wheelmen.

All Victors are fitted with the incomparable Victor Pneumatic Tire, the only tire removable through a hole in the rim.

Victor material and workmanship the best throughout—the highest possible grade.

The best line of saddles ever placed on a bicycle. Don't fail to examine the new Victoria tilting saddle for ladies' use. It solves the problem of an easy mount, and is sure to create a sensation.

The standard price of Victors is $125.00. We were the first leading makers to make this reduced price, and as usual made the pace which others have been obliged to follow.

Victors remain the leading high grade bicycles of the world, and if you want to ride the **BEST** it must be a Victor.

Apply to any Victor agent for Victor catalog, or send a postal direct.

OVERMAN WHEEL CO.

BOSTON.	PHILADELPHIA.	DETROIT.
NEW YORK.	CHICAGO.	DENVER.
	SAN FRANCISCO.	

Bibliography

Duncan, John E. BIKES AND TRIKES OF LONG AGO. American Review, 1975.

Ficther, George, and Kingbay, Keith. BICYCLING. Golden Press, 1972.

Kingbay, Keith. INSIDE BICYCLING. Regnery, 1976.

Leonard, Irving A. WHEN BIKEHOOD WAS IN FLOWER. Bearcamp Press, 1969.

Sloane, Eugene A. THE COMPLETE BOOK OF BICYCLING. Trident Press, 1970.

Sumner, Philip Lawton. EARLY BICYCLES. Evelyn Press, 1966.

Woodforde, John. THE STORY OF THE BICYCLE. Universe Books, 1971.